What some are saying about
Marie and "The RecordKeeper"

Marie Neder has created an excellent health journal, helpful for keeping track of pain, sleep, weight, diet, exercise, and more. As a physical therapist I strongly encourage all of us to keep a health journal, documenting our medications, surgical procedures, vaccinations etc. In addition, keeping track of specific issues, e.g. our pain levels is useful. Our bodies do their best to heal, but not always as fast as we would like. It is helpful to keep track and then to return to our journals to see the progress we have indeed made.

Doranne Long, P.T.

I've appreciated this journal even more than I already thought I would. Being a recently graduated student nurse studying for my state exam this journal helps prevent me from putting my own health on the back burner. Not only has it helped me track my sleeping patterns and eating habits but it has also helped me map out a study plan. I admire all of the photographs and quotes throughout that are inspirational in their own way, leaving room for interpretation by me the reader and being able to apply those thoughts to my day, week, month. I also love the fact that I will be able to look back on these moments in my life referring to times of stress AND joy and my coinciding health patterns. And lastly, it is so helpful to have a place I can record all of my vaccinations as an easy reference for when I start working as a nurse!! Very well put together journal, compliments to the author!

Ashley T, R.N.

The perfect tool to track life patterns of all sorts in an organized and useful format....A great resource for self awareness and health monitoring!

Bartie Hatchman, Ph.D.

This is a straight forward book, practical. It's a way to track your day to day life. For example you'll record choices of what you eat, how you've slept, pain level and exercise. For anyone that needs to stay on top of these daily choices to support their well-being, I think this would be a wonderful tool.

Charlotte Nuessle

The *RecordKeeper* is a wonderful and unique way to journal your feelings, dreams and health all in one book. Your photography interspersed throughout the book is a beautiful and interesting addition. Thank you Marie.

Kathleen Parrott

This is the ideal journal to keep track of all health issues, be aware of your habits and improve one's living. Marie has done an excellent job of helping one to do all this in one book. Her photos and quotes inspire thoughtfulness with beauty. Well done!

Cherilyn M. Peterson

I started my *RecordKeeper* on June 1st. It is a very helpful journal for me to track my various medical and day record of food/drink intake along with exercising that I do. I highly recommend this book for all to keep track of their # one importance of ones health.

Susan Jordan

I love this book and the premise behind it and the awesome woman who wrote and published it! Good for you Marie!! Seeing you being very successful with this.

Jan Albright

The *RecordKeeper* . . . our memories, our moments, expressed in ritual. A great book by an aware lady with a strictly positive impulse. A delightful person . . . a delightful read.

e' bender-webb

The RecordKeeper

Another Pathway to Greater Well-Being

Journaling and Documenting

MARIE C. NEDER

Welcome to a "different" type of journal

The RecordKeeper is my second journal using the same format. I've exchanged the images and quotes, and have included additional pages giving information about journaling and about me.

Along with writing down our feelings, thoughts, dreams and goals, this Record-Keeper also describes what we eat, how we move and what we're feeling. I have been keeping this type of journal for many years and it has served me well. By well I mean I am able to reflect back on a day by day or week by week, or even a month by month basis, allowing me to see what changes I may want to make.
Areas I want to increase like exercise, for example, and areas I may want to limit, like chocolate or alcohol, and so on.

This RecordKeeper encourages you to be as detailed or vague as you wish. You may want to take your temperature daily or not, but the space is there for you to do so. Writing down what you ate that morning might direct you to what you may want to eat the rest of the day in order to eat in a healthy and balanced way.

By all means continue to write down your hopes, dreams, feelings, thoughts, goals. By writing these things down it lends itself to becoming a reality from the written word.

Include affirmations, clip out a favorite image and paste it into your RecordKeeper.

Write with a different colored pen or pencil.
Gosh, the sky is the limit!

This is your RecordKeeper. Treat it with lovingkindness.

For your greatest well-being,

Marie

Let's Get Started...

How to use this RecordKeeper

This RecordKeeper is easy to use. I start each morning with my cup of coffee, a pen and this journal. Morning writings notated below. The other writings can be done throughout the day or near the end of your day.

The following is an explanation for the categories written on each page:

Date: Current date.

Time: The time you got out of bed.

Temp: Your temperature upon arising.

BM: Bowel movement, write down the time of day for each one. If none, write zero.

Scale: On a scale of 1-10 (10 being the best) write in how your total day was.

Sleep: Scale of 1-10 how did you sleep the night before. Record in the morning.

RX: Write down any medications you don't normally take and how much.

CC: Chief Complaint. What, if anything, was bothering you upon rising or throughout the day. Headache? Nausea?

                Jot it down.

Weight: Upon rising. After you use the toilet and without clothes.

BP: Blood pressure readings (and pulse if your cuff includes it) There is space for more than one reading. Any time.

Food & Drink: Write down what you ate and drank throughout the day.

Exercises: Write down what you did – a walk, gardening, weights, etc. and how much time for each activity.

Pain: After exercising was there any pain? Again 1-10 scale.

You get the idea. I love having the time to journal and reflect.

The empty space is for you to write down your dreams, thoughts, feelings and everything else!

Enjoy.

SUN APRIL FOOL'S DAY
EASTER SUNDAY

Date 4-1-18   Scale: 7.3 Sleep 7.5 Weight: 139.0

Time/Temp: 8:03AM, 97.0   CC: Ⓛ hip & leg pain

BM: 8:03AM, 10:35PM   BP: 12:06AM = 132/80, 63

Rx: ½ pain 1pm, ½ pain 10pm

Food/Drink:

B Coffee
1 Hard boiled egg
MIXED FRUIT

Snack:
piece of ham
glass champagne

Dinner:
HAM
3 bean salad
steamed veggies
MIXED Fruit
P. salad
glass champagne

Exercises:

TODAY I
WALKED
2 miles
on easy
trail —
took photos
too!
2½ hours

Pain level post exercise: 3

Notes:

Slept well once I got to sleep!
Awoke to a sunny day.
E, Sue and I attended an
Easter service. It was very
mellow and we each placed
flowers on a cross. Je,
the cross was very colorful
and a little messy — all
the more poignant.
Took Sue home, then she
and her husband Paul
came over to E's house
and we had dinner on
the patio area of his
backyard. Yummy food
and good conversation.
I enjoyed the day,
even with my left
leg and hip slow to
heal. I keep smiling.
I'm no fool ☺

Herstory (Marie's)

Like all of us, I, too, have a story.

I was born by the San Diego sea in Ninety Hundred and Fifty Three. As the daughter of a military father (Navy) we frequently moved. I attended numerous elementary schools – cannot remember how many but I know it was in Rhode Island, California and Washington. I was always the "new kid" in the classroom! However I learned to "swim and not sink!"

My dad retired from the Navy when I was 13 years of age and he was only 37 at the time, young enough to have a second career (V.A. Administration). I only attended two junior high schools and one (yes, one!) high school. After graduating high school I lived in various places in Southern California and also in Washington. I obtained my A.A./B.A. degrees while living in the San Fernando Valley.

I have traveled abroad to places like Europe, the Mediterranean, Hawaii and later to New Zealand and Dubai. I don't believe I've put away my traveling shoes just yet.

After the death of both parents (one in 1997 and the other in 2003) I moved to Grants Pass, Oregon where I have lived for the past 12 ½ years.

Fast forward to June of 2009 where I discovered a lump on my neck (the right side) and was diagnosed with Non Hodgkin's Lymphoma (Stage 3!) and underwent chemo therapy. Yes, I lost my hair everywhere on the body, even in my nose! While undergoing treatment I was encouraged not only to journal (which I kept for many years) but to write copious notes on how I was feeling, how I slept, what I ate and so on. Well, after passing my 5-year benchmark, which meant that I was "cured" of this disease, I was so thoroughly entrenched in writing in my journal that I just kept writing; writing detailed notes, thoughts, observations and more. Thus in 2017 I self-published "The RecordKeeper," certainly much more than a journal.

For your greatest well-being,

Marie

"The arch at Endarts"

Here we go...

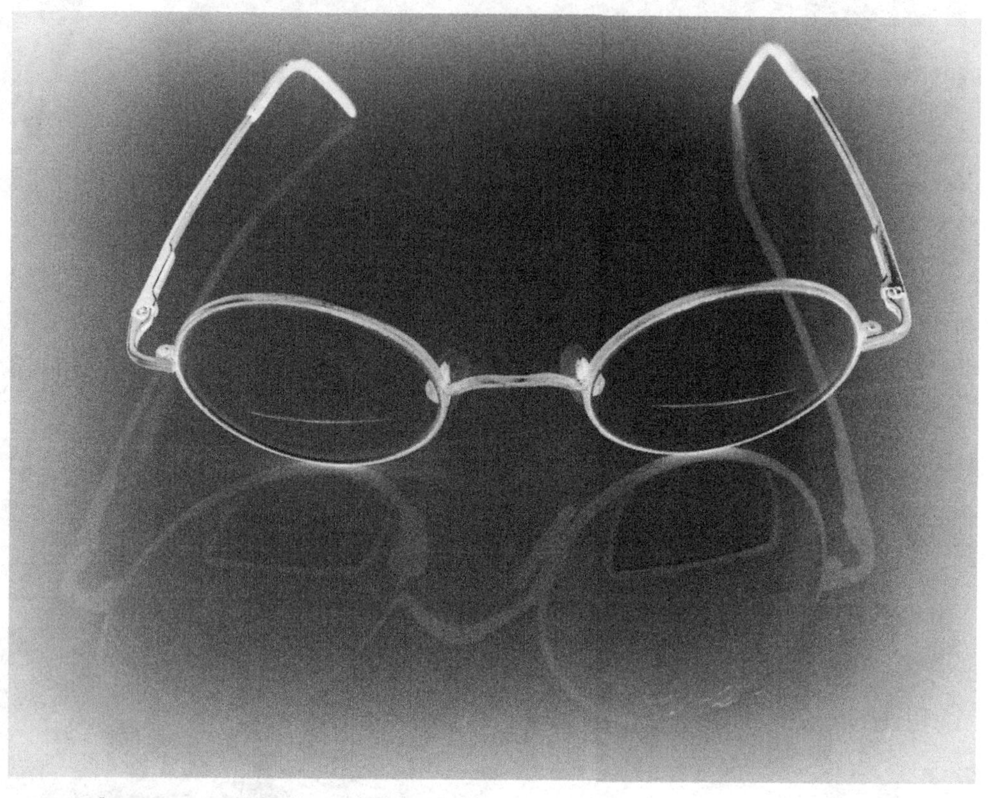

"The man who does not read has no advantage over the man who cannot read."
—Mark Twain

Just for today I am thankful for

____

Date _________

Scale: ______ Sleep ______ Weight:______

Time/Temp: _________________

CC: _____________________________

BM: _____________________________

BP: _____________________________

Rx: _____________________________

Food/Drink:

Notes:

Exercises:

Pain level
post exercise: ______

Date _________

Scale: _____ Sleep ______ Weight:______

Time/Temp: _________________

CC: _____________________________

BM: _______________________________

BP: _________________________

Rx: _________________________

Food/Drink:

Notes:

____

____

____

____

____

____

____

____

____

____

____

____

____

____

____

____

____

____

____

____

Exercises:

Pain level
post exercise: _____

Date _________

Scale: ______ Sleep _______ Weight:_______

Time/Temp: ________________

CC: ___________________________

BM: ______________________________

BP: _____________________________

Rx: _____________________________

Food/Drink:

Notes:

____

____

____

____

____

____

____

____

____

____

____

____

____

____

____

____

____

____

____

Exercises:

Pain level
post exercise: ______

Date ________   Scale: _____ Sleep ______ Weight:______

Time/Temp: ______________   CC: ______________________

BM: _____________________   BP: ________________________

Rx: ________________________

Food/Drink: *Notes:*

Exercises:

Pain level
post exercise: _____

Date _________

Scale: ______   Sleep _______   Weight:_______

Time/Temp: __________________

CC: _________________________________

BM: ______________________________

BP: _________________________________

Rx: _________________________________

Food/Drink:

Notes:

____

____

____

____

____

____

____

____

____

____

____

____

Exercises:

____

____

____

____

____

____

____

____

**Pain level
post exercise:** ______

____

Date _________

Scale: _____ Sleep ______ Weight:______

Time/Temp: ________________

CC: ____________________________

BM: ___________________________

BP: _____________________________

Rx: _____________________________

Food/Drink:

Notes:

____

____

____

____

____

____

____

____

____

____

____

____

____

____

____

____

____

____

____

____

Exercises:

Pain level
post exercise: _____

Date _________

Scale: ______   Sleep _______   Weight:_______

Time/Temp: _________________

CC: ____________________________

BM: ____________________________

BP: _______________________________

Rx: _______________________________

Food/Drink:

Notes:

Exercises:

Pain level
post exercise: ______

Date _________

Scale: _____ Sleep ______ Weight:______

Time/Temp: _______________

CC: ___________________________

BM: ______________________________

BP: ____________________________

Rx: ____________________________

Notes:

____

____

____

____

____

____

____

____

____

____

____

____

____

____

____

____

____

____

____

____

____

Date _________

Scale: ______   Sleep _______ Weight:_______

Time/Temp: ________________

CC: ___________________________

BM: _______________________________

BP: ____________________________

Rx: ____________________________

Food/Drink:

Notes:

____

____

____

____

____

____

____

____

____

____

____

____

____

____

____

____

____

____

____

____

____

Exercises:

Pain level
post exercise: ______

"A friend is someone who knows all about you and still loves you."
—Elbert Hubbard

Just for today I am thankful for

____

Date _________

Scale: ______ Sleep _______ Weight:_______

Time/Temp: _________________

CC: _____________________________

BM: _______________________________

BP: _______________________________

Rx: _______________________________

Food/Drink:

Notes:

____

____

____

____

____

____

____

____

____

____

____

____

____

____

____

____

____

____

____

____

Exercises:

Pain level
post exercise: ______

Date _________

Scale: _____ Sleep _______ Weight:______

Time/Temp: _________________

CC: ___________________________

BM: _________________________

BP: ___________________________

Rx: ___________________________

Food/Drink:

Notes:

____

____

____

____

____

____

____

____

____

____

____

____

____

____

____

____

____

Exercises:

____

____

____

____

____

Pain level
post exercise: _____

____

Date _________

Scale: ______ Sleep _______ Weight:_______

Time/Temp: ________________________

CC: ________________________________

BM: _______________________________

BP: ________________________________

Rx: ________________________________

Food/Drink:

Notes:

____

____

____

____

____

____

____

____

____

____

____

____

____

____

____

____

____

____

____

Exercises:

Pain level
post exercise: ______

Date _________

Scale: _____ Sleep ______ Weight:______

Time/Temp: ________________

CC: ______________________________

BM: ______________________________

BP: ______________________________

Rx: ______________________________

Food/Drink:

Notes:

____

____

____

____

____

____

____

____

____

____

____

Exercises:

____

____

____

____

____

____

____

____

____

Pain level
post exercise: _____

____

Date ________

Scale: _____ Sleep ______ Weight:______

Time/Temp: ________________

CC: __________________________

BM: _________________________

BP: _________________________

Rx: _________________________

Food/Drink:

Notes:

Exercises:

**Pain level
post exercise:** _____

Date _________

Scale: _____ Sleep ______ Weight:______

Time/Temp: ________________

CC: ____________________________

BM: _______________________________

BP: ______________________________

Rx: _______________________________

Food/Drink:

Notes:

____

____

____

____

____

____

____

____

____

____

____

____

____

____

____

____

____

____

____

Exercises:

Pain level
post exercise: _____

Date _________

Scale: ______   Sleep ______   Weight:______

Time/Temp: ________________

CC: ___________________________

BM: _________________________

BP: ___________________________

Rx: ___________________________

Food/Drink:

Notes:

____

____

____

____

____

____

____

____

____

____

____

____

Exercises:

____

____

____

____

____

____

____

____

____

Pain level
post exercise: ______

____

Date ________

Scale: _____ Sleep ______ Weight:______

Time/Temp: __________________

CC: ____________________________

BM: ___________________________

BP: ____________________________

Rx: ____________________________

Food/Drink:

Notes:

____
____
____
____
____
____
____
____
____
____
____
____
____
____
____
____
____
____
____
____

Exercises:

Pain level
post exercise: _____

Date ________

Scale: _____   Sleep ______   Weight:______

Time/Temp: _______________

CC: ______________________

BM: ______________________

BP: ____________________

Rx: ____________________

Food/Drink:

Notes:

Exercises:

Pain level
post exercise: _____

"Not all of us can do great things.
But we can do small things with great love."
—Mother Teresa

Just for today I am thankful for

____

Date _________

Scale: ______ Sleep _______ Weight:_______

Time/Temp: _________________

CC: _________________________

BM: _______________________

BP: _________________________

Rx: _________________________

Notes:

____
____
____
____
____
____
____
____
____
____
____
____
____
____
____
____
____
____
____

Date _________

Scale: _____ Sleep _______ Weight:______

Time/Temp: ________________

CC: _____________________________

BM: ____________________________

BP: _____________________________

Rx: _____________________________

Food/Drink:

Notes:

____

____

____

____

____

____

____

____

____

____

____

____

____

____

____

____

____

____

____

____

Exercises:

Pain level
post exercise: _____

Date _________

Scale: _____ Sleep _____ Weight:______

Time/Temp: ________________

CC: ____________________________

BM: ______________________________

BP: ______________________________

Rx: ______________________________

Food/Drink:

Notes:

____

____

____

____

____

____

____

____

____

____

Exercises:

____

____

____

____

____

____

____

____

____

____

____

**Pain level
post exercise:** _____

____

Date _________

Scale: ______ Sleep _______ Weight:______

Time/Temp: ________________

CC: ____________________________

BM: ________________________________

BP: __________________________________

Rx: ____________________________

Food/Drink:

Notes:

Exercises:

Pain level
post exercise: _____

Date ________

Scale: _____ Sleep _____ Weight:_____

Time/Temp: _______________

CC: _______________________

BM: _______________________

BP: _______________________

Rx: _______________________

Food/Drink:

Notes:

Exercises:

Pain level
post exercise: _____

Date _______

Scale: _____ Sleep ______ Weight:______

Time/Temp: _________________

CC: ___________________________

BM: _______________________________

BP: ____________________________

Rx: ____________________________

Food/Drink:

Notes:

____

____

____

____

____

____

____

____

____

____

____

____

____

____

____

____

Exercises:

____

____

____

____

Pain level
post exercise: _____

Date _________

Scale: ______ Sleep _______ Weight:_______

Time/Temp: _________________

CC: _____________________________

BM: _______________________________

BP: _______________________________

Rx: _______________________________

Food/Drink:

Notes:

____

____

____

____

____

____

____

____

____

____

____

____

____

Exercises:

____

____

____

____

____

____

____

____

Pain level
post exercise: ______

____

Date _________

Scale: ______ Sleep _______ Weight:_______

Time/Temp: __________________

CC: ______________________________

BM: ______________________________

BP: ______________________________

Rx: ______________________________

Food/Drink:

Notes:

____

____

____

____

____

____

____

____

____

____

____

____

____

____

____

____

____

____

____

____

Exercises:

Pain level
post exercise: ______

Date _________

Scale: _____   Sleep ______   Weight:______

Time/Temp: _________________

CC: _______________________________

BM: _______________________________

BP: _______________________________

Rx: _______________________________

Food/Drink:

Notes:

____

____

____

____

____

____

____

____

____

____

____

____

____

Exercises:

____

____

____

____

____

____

____

**Pain level
post exercise:** _____

____

"Some day you will be old enough to start reading fairy tales again."
—C.S. Lewis

Just for today I am thankful for

____

Date _______

Scale: _____ Sleep ______ Weight:______

Time/Temp: ________________

CC: ____________________________

BM: _______________________

BP: ____________________________

Rx: ____________________________

Food/Drink:

Notes:

____

____

____

____

____

____

____

____

____

____

____

Exercises:

____

____

____

____

____

____

____

____

____

Pain level
post exercise: _____

____

Date _________

Scale: _____ Sleep _______ Weight:______

Time/Temp: ________________

CC: ___________________________

BM: ___________________________

BP: ___________________________

Rx: ___________________________

Food/Drink:

Notes:

____

____

____

____

____

____

____

____

____

____

____

____

____

____

____

____

____

____

____

____

____

Exercises:

**Pain level
post exercise:** _____

Date _________

Scale: _____ Sleep ______ Weight:______

Time/Temp: _______________

CC: _____________________________

BM: ______________________________

BP: _______________________________

Rx: _______________________________

Food/Drink:

Notes:

____

____

____

____

____

____

____

____

____

____

Exercises:

____

____

____

____

____

____

____

Pain level
post exercise: _____

____

Date _________

Time/Temp: _______________

BM: _______________________

Scale: ______ Sleep _______ Weight:______

CC: _______________________

BP: _______________________

Rx: _______________________

Food/Drink:

Notes:

____

____

____

____

____

____

____

____

____

____

____

____

____

____

____

____

____

____

____

____

____

Exercises:

Pain level
post exercise: ______

Date _________

Scale: _____ Sleep ______ Weight:______

Time/Temp: _______________

CC: ___________________________

BM: ____________________________

BP: ____________________________

Rx: ____________________________

Food/Drink:

Notes:

____

____

____

____

____

____

____

____

____

____

____

____

____

____

____

____

____

____

____

____

Exercises:

Pain level
post exercise: _____

Date _________

Scale: _____ Sleep ______ Weight:______

Time/Temp: ________________

CC: ___________________________

BM: ____________________________

BP: ___________________________

Rx: ___________________________

Notes:

____
____
____
____
____
____
____
____
____
____
____
____
____
____
____
____
____
____
____
____
____
____

Date ________

Scale: ______ Sleep ______ Weight:______

Time/Temp: _______________

CC: ___________________________

BM: ______________________________

BP: _____________________________

Rx: _____________________________

Food/Drink:

Notes:

____

____

____

____

____

____

____

____

____

____

____

____

Exercises:

____

____

____

____

____

____

____

____

____

Pain level
post exercise: ______

____

Date _________

Scale: ______ Sleep _______ Weight:______

Time/Temp: ________________

CC: _____________________________

BM: ________________________

BP: _____________________________

Rx: _____________________________

Notes:

____

____

____

____

____

____

____

____

____

____

____

____

____

____

____

____

____

____

____

____

Exercises:

Pain level
post exercise: ______

Date _________

Scale: ______ Sleep _______ Weight:_______

Time/Temp: _________________

CC: _______________________________

BM: _______________________________

BP: _______________________________

Rx: _______________________________

Food/Drink:

Notes:

____

____

____

____

____

____

____

____

____

____

____

____

____

____

____

____

____

____

____

____

Exercises:

Pain level
post exercise: ______

A person's a person, no matter how small."
—Dr. Seuss, *Horton Hears a Who!*

Just for today I am thankful for

____

Date ________

Scale: _____ Sleep ______ Weight:______

Time/Temp: ________________

CC: ____________________________

BM: ______________________________

BP: ____________________________

Rx: ____________________________

Food/Drink:

Notes:

____

____

____

____

____

____

____

____

____

____

____

____

Exercises:

____

____

____

____

____

____

____

Pain level
post exercise: _____

____

Date _________

Scale: ______ Sleep _______ Weight:______

Time/Temp: _________________

CC: __________________________

BM: _____________________________

BP: ___________________________

Rx: ___________________________

Food/Drink:

Notes:

____

____

____

____

____

____

____

____

____

____

____

____

____

____

____

____

____

____

____

Exercises:

Pain level
post exercise: ______

Date _________

Scale: ______ Sleep _______ Weight:_______

Time/Temp: _________________

CC: _____________________________

BM: _______________________________

BP: _______________________________

Rx: _____________________________

Food/Drink:

Notes:

____

____

____

____

____

____

____

____

____

____

____

____

____

____

____

____

____

____

Exercises:

____

____

Pain level
post exercise: ______

Date _________

Scale: ______   Sleep _______   Weight:______

Time/Temp: _________________

CC: _____________________________

BM: _______________________________

BP: _______________________________

Rx: _______________________________

Food/Drink:

Notes:

____
____
____
____
____
____
____
____
____
____
____
____
____
____
____
____
____
____
____
____
____

Exercises:

Pain level
post exercise: ______

Date _________

Scale: ______   Sleep _______   Weight:_______

Time/Temp: __________________

CC: _______________________________

BM: _______________________________

BP: _______________________________

Rx: _______________________________

Food/Drink:

Notes:

____

____

____

____

____

____

____

____

____

____

____

Exercises:

____

____

____

____

____

____

____

Pain level
post exercise: ______

____

Date ________

Scale: _____ Sleep _____ Weight:_____

Time/Temp: ________________

CC: ______________________

BM: ____________________

BP: _______________________

Rx: ______________________

Food/Drink:

Notes:

____

____

____

____

____

____

____

____

____

____

Exercises:

____

____

____

____

____

____

____

____

Pain level
post exercise: _____

____

Date _________

Scale: _____ Sleep ______ Weight:______

Time/Temp: _______________

CC: _______________________

BM: ____________________________

BP: ___________________________

Rx: ___________________________

Food/Drink:

Notes:

____

____

____

____

____

____

____

____

____

____

____

____

____

____

____

____

____

____

____

Exercises:

____

____

Pain level
post exercise: _____

Date _________

Scale: _____ Sleep ______ Weight:______

Time/Temp: _________________

CC: ____________________________

BM: _______________________________

BP: _____________________________

Rx: _____________________________

Food/Drink:

Notes:

Exercises:

Pain level
post exercise: _____

Date ________

Scale: _____ Sleep ______ Weight:______

Time/Temp: _______________

CC: ____________________

BM: ___________________________

BP: ____________________

Rx: ____________________

Food/Drink:

Notes:

____

____

____

____

____

____

____

____

____

____

____

____

____

____

____

____

____

____

____

Exercises:

Pain level
post exercise: _____

*"And hand in hand, on the edge of the sand, they danced
by the light of the moon."*
—Edward Lear, *The Owl and the Pussycat*

Just for today I am thankful for

____

Date ________

Scale: _____ Sleep ______ Weight:______

Time/Temp: ________________

CC: ____________________________

BM: ___________________________

BP: __________________________

Rx: ________________________

Food/Drink:

Notes:

Exercises:

Pain level
post exercise: _____

Date _________

Scale: ______ Sleep _______ Weight:_______

Time/Temp: _________________

CC: _____________________________

BM: _____________________________

BP: _____________________________

Rx: _____________________________

Food/Drink:

Notes:

____

____

____

____

____

____

____

____

____

____

____

____

____

____

____

____

____

____

____

____

____

Exercises:

Pain level
post exercise: ______

Date ________

Scale: _____ Sleep _____ Weight:_____

Time/Temp: _______________

CC: _______________________

BM: _______________________

BP: _______________________

Rx: _______________________

Food/Drink:

Notes:

Exercises:

Pain level
post exercise: _____

Date _________

Scale: _____ Sleep ______ Weight:______

Time/Temp: ________________

CC: ___________________________

BM: _______________________

BP: ______________________________

Rx: ______________________________

Food/Drink:

Notes:

____

____

____

____

____

____

____

____

____

____

____

____

____

____

____

____

____

____

____

Exercises:

Pain level
post exercise: _____

Date _________

Scale: _____ Sleep ______ Weight:______

Time/Temp: ________________

CC: ___________________________

BM: _____________________________

BP: ____________________________

Rx: ____________________________

Food/Drink:

Notes:

____

____

____

____

____

____

____

____

____

____

____

Exercises:

____

____

____

____

____

____

____

____

**Pain level
post exercise:** _____

____

Date ________

Scale: _____ Sleep ______ Weight:______

Time/Temp: _______________

CC: _______________________

BM: ________________________

BP: ________________________

Rx: ______________________

Food/Drink:

Notes:

Exercises:

**Pain level
post exercise:** _____

Date _________

Scale: _____   Sleep ______   Weight:______

Time/Temp: _______________

CC: ______________________________

BM: _______________________

BP: ______________________________

Rx: ______________________________

Food/Drink:

Notes:

____

____

____

____

____

____

____

____

____

____

____

____

Exercises:

____

____

____

____

____

____

____

Pain level
post exercise: _____

____

Date ________

Time/Temp: _________________

BM: _______________________

Scale: _____ Sleep ______ Weight:______

CC: ___________________________

BP: __________________________

Rx: _________________________

Food/Drink:

Exercises:

Pain level
post exercise: _____

Notes:

____

____

____

____

____

____

____

____

____

____

____

____

____

____

____

____

____

____

____

____

Date _________

Scale: _____ Sleep ______ Weight:______

Time/Temp: _______________

CC: ____________________________

BM: ____________________________

BP: _______________________

Rx: _______________________

Food/Drink:

Notes:

____

____

____

____

____

____

____

____

____

____

____

____

____

____

____

____

____

____

____

____

Exercises:

Pain level
post exercise: _____

From the beneath the soil . . .

Just for today I am thankful for

____

Date ________

Scale: _____ Sleep ______ Weight:______

Time/Temp: ________________

CC: _________________________

BM: ________________________

BP: _______________________

Rx: _______________________

Food/Drink:

Notes:

Exercises:

Pain level
post exercise: _____

Date _________

Scale: _____   Sleep ______   Weight:______

Time/Temp: ________________

CC: _______________________

BM: ____________________________

BP: ____________________________

Rx: ____________________________

Food/Drink:

Notes:

____

____

____

____

____

____

____

____

____

____

____

____

____

____

____

____

____

____

____

Exercises:

Pain level
post exercise: _____

Date _________

Scale: ______ Sleep _______ Weight:______

Time/Temp: __________________

CC: ___________________________

BM: _______________________

BP: ____________________________

Rx: ____________________________

Food/Drink:

Notes:

____

____

____

____

____

____

____

____

____

____

Exercises:

____

____

____

____

____

____

____

____

____

____

**Pain level
post exercise:** ______

____

Date _________

Scale: ______ Sleep _______ Weight:_______

Time/Temp: _________________

CC: _______________________________

BM: ____________________________

BP: _______________________________

Rx: _______________________________

Food/Drink:

Notes:

____

____

____

____

____

____

____

____

____

____

____

Exercises:

____

____

____

____

____

____

____

____

____

Pain level
post exercise: ______

____

Date _________

Scale: ______ Sleep _______ Weight:______

Time/Temp: ________________

CC: _______________________

BM: ___________________________

BP: _________________________

Rx: _________________________

Notes:

____

____

____

____

____

____

____

____

____

____

____

____

____

____

____

____

____

____

____

____

Exercises:

Pain level
post exercise: ______

Date ________

Scale: _____   Sleep ______   Weight:______

Time/Temp: _______________

CC: ________________________

BM: ______________________

BP: ______________________

Rx: ______________________

Food/Drink:

Exercises:

Pain level
post exercise: _____

Notes:

Date _________

Scale: _____ Sleep _____ Weight: _____

Time/Temp: _______________

CC: ____________________

BM: ____________________

BP: ____________________

Rx: ____________________

Food/Drink:

Notes:

____

____

____

____

____

____

____

____

____

____

Exercises:

____

____

____

____

____

____

____

____

____

Pain level
post exercise: _____

____

Date _________

Scale: _____ Sleep ______ Weight:______

Time/Temp: ________________

CC: ____________________________

BM: ______________________________

BP: ____________________________

Rx: ____________________________

Food/Drink:

Notes:

____

____

____

____

____

____

____

____

____

____

____

____

Exercises:

____

____

____

____

____

____

____

____

Pain level
post exercise: _____

____

Date _________

Scale: ______   Sleep _______   Weight:______

Time/Temp: ________________

CC: _____________________

BM: _____________________

BP: ______________________

Rx: ______________________

Food/Drink:

Notes:

____

____

____

____

____

____

____

____

____

____

____

____

____

____

____

____

____

____

Exercises:

Pain level
post exercise: ______

____

"The desire to reach for the stars is ambitious.
The desire to reach hearts is wise."
—Maya Angelou

Just for today I am thankful for

____

Date _________

Scale: _____ Sleep ______ Weight:______

Time/Temp: _______________

CC: ___________________________

BM: ________________________

BP: ____________________________

Rx: ____________________________

Food/Drink:

Notes:

Exercises:

Pain level
post exercise: ______

Date _________

Scale: ______   Sleep _______   Weight:______

Time/Temp: _________________

CC: _______________________________

BM: _______________________________

BP: _________________________________

Rx: ________________________________

Food/Drink:

Notes:

____
____
____
____
____
____
____
____
____
____
____
____
____
____
____
____
____
____
____

Exercises:

Pain level
post exercise: _____

Date _________

Scale: _____ Sleep ______ Weight:______

Time/Temp: _______________

CC: _____________________________

BM: _____________________________

BP: _____________________________

Rx: _____________________________

Food/Drink:

Notes:

____

____

____

____

____

____

____

____

____

____

____

____

____

____

____

____

____

____

Exercises:

____

____

____

____

Pain level
post exercise: _____

Date ________

Scale: _____   Sleep ______   Weight:_____

Time/Temp: ________________

CC: ______________________

BM: ______________________

BP: ____________________

Rx: _____________________

Food/Drink:

Notes:

____

____

____

____

____

____

____

____

____

Exercises:

____

____

____

____

____

____

____

**Pain level
post exercise:** _____

____

Date _________

Scale: _____ Sleep ______ Weight:______

Time/Temp: ________________

CC: _____________________________

BM: ___________________________

BP: _______________________________

Rx: _______________________________

Food/Drink:

Notes:

____

____

____

____

____

____

____

____

____

____

____

Exercises:

____

____

____

____

____

____

____

____

____

Pain level
post exercise: _____

____

Date _________

Scale: _____ Sleep ______ Weight:______

Time/Temp: ________________

CC: ____________________________

BM: _______________________________

BP: _______________________________

Rx: ______________________________

Food/Drink:

Notes:

____

____

____

____

____

____

____

____

____

____

____

Exercises:

____

____

____

____

____

____

____

____

____

Pain level
post exercise: _____

____

Date _________

Scale: ______   Sleep _______   Weight:______

Time/Temp: ________________________

CC: ___________________________________

BM: _______________________________

BP: ___________________________________

Rx: ___________________________________

Food/Drink:

Notes:

____

____

____

____

____

____

____

____

____

____

____

Exercises:

____

____

____

____

____

____

____

____

Pain level
post exercise: ______

____

Date ________

Scale: ______   Sleep ______   Weight: ______

Time/Temp: _________________

CC: __________________________

BM: _____________________________

BP: ___________________________

Rx: ___________________________

Food/Drink:

Notes:

____

____

____

____

____

____

____

____

____

____

____

____

____

____

____

____

____

____

____

Exercises:

Pain level
post exercise: ______

Date _________

Scale: ______ Sleep _______ Weight:_______

Time/Temp: __________________

CC: ____________________________

BM: ____________________________

BP: ____________________________

Rx: ____________________________

Food/Drink:

Notes:

____

____

____

____

____

____

____

____

____

____

____

____

____

____

____

____

____

____

Exercises:

**Pain level
post exercise:** ______

"Fear knocked at the door, Faith answered and nobody was there."
—Unknown

Just for today I am thankful for

____

Date _________

Scale: ______   Sleep _______   Weight:______

Time/Temp: _______________

CC: _____________________________

BM: _____________________________

BP: _____________________________

Rx: _____________________________

Food/Drink:

Notes:

____

____

____

____

____

____

____

____

____

____

____

____

____

____

____

____

____

____

____

____

Exercises:

Pain level
post exercise: ______

Date _________

Scale: ______ Sleep _______ Weight:______

Time/Temp: __________________

CC: _______________________________

BM: _______________________________

BP: _______________________________

Rx: _______________________________

Food/Drink:

Notes:

____

____

____

____

____

____

____

____

____

____

____

____

____

____

____

____

____

____

____

Exercises:

____

____

**Pain level
post exercise:** ______

Date _________

Scale: ______ Sleep _______ Weight:______

Time/Temp: _________________

CC: _____________________________

BM: ____________________________

BP: _____________________________

Rx: _____________________________

Food/Drink:

Notes:

____

____

____

____

____

____

____

____

____

____

____

____

____

____

____

____

____

____

____

____

Exercises:

Pain level
post exercise: ______

Date _________

Scale: _______   Sleep _______   Weight: _______

Time/Temp: _________________

CC: _____________________________

BM: _____________________________

BP: _____________________________

Rx: _____________________________

Notes:

____

____

____

____

____

____

____

____

____

____

____

____

____

____

____

____

____

____

____

Exercises:

Pain level
post exercise: _______

Date ________

Time/Temp: _______________

BM: _______________________

Scale: _____ Sleep ______ Weight:______

CC: ________________________

BP: _______________________

Rx: _______________________

Food/Drink:

Exercises:

Pain level
post exercise: _____

Notes:

Date ________   Scale: _____ Sleep ______ Weight: ______

Time/Temp: _______________   CC: _____________________

BM: _____________________   BP: _____________________

                              Rx: _____________________

Food/Drink: *Notes:*

____

____

____

____

____

____

____

____

____

____

____

____

____

____

____

____

____

____

Exercises:

____

**Pain level
post exercise:** _____

Date _________

Scale: ______ Sleep _______ Weight:______

Time/Temp: ________________

CC: _____________________________

BM: _________________________

BP: _______________________________

Rx: _______________________________

Food/Drink:

Notes:

____

____

____

____

____

____

____

____

____

____

____

____

____

____

Exercises:

____

____

____

____

____

____

____

Pain level
post exercise: ______

Date ________

Scale: _____ Sleep ______ Weight: ______

Time/Temp: __________________

CC: _________________________

BM: ____________________________

BP: ____________________________

Rx: ___________________________

Food/Drink:

Notes:

Exercises:

Pain level
post exercise: _____

Date _________

Scale: _____ Sleep ______ Weight:______

Time/Temp: _______________

CC: ____________________________

BM: _______________________

BP: ____________________________

Rx: ____________________________

Food/Drink:

Notes:

____

____

____

____

____

____

____

____

____

____

____

____

____

Exercises:

____

____

____

____

____

____

____

____

____

Pain level
post exercise: _____

____

"Love is like the wind, you can't see it but you can feel it."
—Nicholas Sparks, *A Walk to Remember*

Just for today I am thankful for

____

Date _________

Scale: _____ Sleep ______ Weight:______

Time/Temp: ________________

CC: ____________________________

BM: ____________________________

BP: ____________________________

Rx: ____________________________

Food/Drink:

Notes:

____

____

____

____

____

____

____

____

____

____

____

____

Exercises:

____

____

____

____

____

____

____

____

Pain level
post exercise: _____

____

Date _________

Scale: _____ Sleep _______ Weight:______

Time/Temp: ________________

CC: _____________________________

BM: _______________________________

BP: _____________________________

Rx: _____________________________

Food/Drink:

Notes:

____

____

____

____

____

____

____

____

____

____

____

____

Exercises:

____

____

____

____

____

____

____

____

____

Pain level
post exercise: _____

____

Date _________

Scale: ______   Sleep _______   Weight:_______

Time/Temp: _________________

CC: ____________________________

BM: _______________________________

BP: _________________________________

Rx: _________________________________

Food/Drink:

Notes:

Exercises:

Pain level
post exercise: _____

Date _________

Scale: _____ Sleep ______ Weight:______

Time/Temp: _________________

CC: _____________________

BM: ____________________

BP: ___________________

Rx: ___________________

Food/Drink:

Notes:

____

____

____

____

____

____

____

____

____

____

Exercises:

____

____

____

____

____

____

____

____

____

Pain level
post exercise: _____

____

Date _________

Scale: _____ Sleep ______ Weight:______

Time/Temp: _______________

CC: ____________________________

BM: ______________________________

BP: _____________________________

Rx: _____________________________

Food/Drink:

Notes:

____

____

____

____

____

____

____

____

____

____

Exercises:

____

____

____

____

____

____

____

____

____

Pain level
post exercise: _____

____

Date _________

Scale: ______ Sleep _______ Weight:_______

Time/Temp: ________________

CC: ____________________________

BM: ______________________________

BP: ______________________________

Rx: ____________________________

Food/Drink:

Notes:

____

____

____

____

____

____

____

____

____

____

____

Exercises:

____

____

____

____

____

____

____

____

Pain level
post exercise: ______

____

____

Date _________

Scale: ______ Sleep _______ Weight:_______

Time/Temp: ________________

CC: ______________________________

BM: ______________________________

BP: ______________________________

Rx: ______________________________

Food/Drink:

Notes:

Exercises:

Pain level
post exercise: ______

Date _________

Scale: _____ Sleep ______ Weight:______

Time/Temp: ________________

CC: ___________________________

BM: ______________________________

BP: _______________________________

Rx: _______________________________

Food/Drink:

Notes:

____

____

____

____

____

____

____

____

____

____

____

____

Exercises:

____

____

____

____

____

____

____

____

Pain level
post exercise: _____

____

Date ________

Scale: _____ Sleep _____ Weight:______

Time/Temp: ______________

CC: ________________________

BM: ___________________________

BP: _________________________

Rx: _______________________

Food/Drink:

Notes:

Exercises:

Pain level
post exercise: _____

*"I can't change the direction of the wind, but I can adjust my sails
to always reach my destination."*
—Jimmy Dean, Singer, 1928-2010

Just for today I am thankful for

____

Date _________

Scale: ______   Sleep _______   Weight: ______

Time/Temp: _________________

CC: _______________________________

BM: _______________________________

BP: _______________________________

Rx: _______________________________

Food/Drink:

Notes:

____

____

____

____

____

____

____

____

____

____

____

____

Exercises:

____

____

____

____

____

____

____

____

Pain level
post exercise: _____

____

Date _________

Scale: _____ Sleep _____ Weight: _____

Time/Temp: _________________

CC: _____________________

BM: _____________________

BP: _____________________

Rx: _____________________

Food/Drink:

Notes:

____

____

____

____

____

____

____

____

____

____

____

____

____

____

____

____

____

____

____

____

____

Exercises:

Pain level
post exercise: _____

Date ________

Scale: _____ Sleep ______ Weight:______

Time/Temp: ________________

CC: ____________________________

BM: ________________________

BP: ____________________________

Rx: ____________________________

Food/Drink:

Notes:

____

____

____

____

____

____

____

____

____

____

____

____

____

____

____

____

____

____

____

____

____

____

Exercises:

Pain level
post exercise: _____

Date ________

Scale: _____ Sleep ______ Weight:______

Time/Temp: ________________

CC: _________________________

BM: ____________________________

BP: _________________________

Rx: _________________________

Food/Drink:

Notes:

Exercises:

Pain level
post exercise: _____

Date _________

Scale: ______ Sleep ______ Weight:______

Time/Temp: _______________

CC: _____________________

BM: _______________________

BP: _____________________

Rx: _____________________

Food/Drink:

Notes:

____

Exercises:

Pain level
post exercise: ______

Date _________

Scale: _______ Sleep _______ Weight:_______

Time/Temp: ___________________

CC: _______________________________

BM: _________________________________

BP: _________________________________

Rx: _________________________________

Food/Drink:

Notes:

____

____

____

____

____

____

____

____

____

____

____

____

____

____

____

____

____

____

____

____

Exercises:

Pain level
post exercise: _____

Date ________

Scale: _____   Sleep ______   Weight:______

Time/Temp: _______________

CC: ________________________

BM: _______________________

BP: ______________________

Rx: ______________________

Food/Drink:

Notes:

Exercises:

Pain level
post exercise: _____

Date ________   Scale: _____ Sleep ______ Weight:______

Time/Temp: ________________   CC: _______________________

BM: _______________________   BP: ______________________

Rx: ______________________

Food/Drink: *Notes:*

Exercises:

Pain level
post exercise: _____

Date ________

Scale: _____ Sleep ______ Weight:______

Time/Temp: _________________

CC: ___________________________

BM: _______________________________

BP: ___________________________

Rx: ___________________________

Food/Drink:

Notes:

____

____

____

____

____

____

____

____

____

____

____

____

____

____

____

____

____

____

____

____

____

Exercises:

Pain level
post exercise: _____

"If you cannot be a poet, be the poem."
—David Carradine

Just for today I am thankful for

____

Date _________

Scale: _____   Sleep ______   Weight:______

Time/Temp: _______________   CC: _____________________________

BM: ___________________________   BP: _______________________________

Rx: _____________________________

Food/Drink:

Notes:

____

____

____

____

____

____

____

____

____

____

____

Exercises:

____

____

____

____

____

____

____

____

____

Pain level
post exercise: _____

____

Date _________

Scale: ______   Sleep ______   Weight:______

Time/Temp: _________________

CC: ____________________________

BM: _________________________

BP: ____________________________

Rx: ____________________________

Food/Drink:

Notes:

____

____

____

____

____

____

____

____

____

____

Exercises:

____

____

____

____

____

____

____

____

____

____

Pain level
post exercise: _____

____

Date _________

Scale: _____ Sleep ______ Weight:______

Time/Temp: ________________

CC: ___________________________

BM: ____________________________

BP: ___________________________

Rx: ___________________________

Food/Drink:

Notes:

____

____

____

____

____

____

____

____

____

____

____

Exercises:

____

____

____

____

____

____

____

____

Pain level
post exercise: _____

____

Date _________

Scale: ______ Sleep _______ Weight:______

Time/Temp: ________________

CC: ____________________

BM: ____________________

BP: ____________________

Rx: ____________________

Food/Drink:

Notes:

____

____

____

____

____

____

____

____

____

____

____

____

____

____

____

____

____

____

____

____

Exercises:

Pain level
post exercise: _____

Date ________

Scale: _____ Sleep ______ Weight:______

Time/Temp: ________________

CC: _________________________

BM: _________________________

BP: _________________________

Rx: ______________________

Food/Drink:

Notes:

Exercises:

**Pain level
post exercise:** _____

Date _________

Scale: _____ Sleep ______ Weight:______

Time/Temp: _______________

CC: _____________________

BM: ______________________

BP: ______________________

Rx: ______________________

Notes:

____

____

____

____

____

____

____

____

____

____

____

____

____

____

____

____

____

____

____

____

Date _________

Scale: ______ Sleep _______ Weight:_______

Time/Temp: __________________

CC: ___________________________

BM: ________________________

BP: _____________________________

Rx: _____________________________

Food/Drink:

Notes:

____

____

____

____

____

____

____

____

____

____

____

____

____

____

____

____

____

Exercises:

____

____

____

Pain level
post exercise: ______

Date _______

Scale: _____ Sleep ______ Weight:______

Time/Temp: _______________

CC: ___________________________

BM: _______________________

BP: ____________________________

Rx: ____________________________

Food/Drink:

Notes:

____

____

____

____

____

____

____

____

____

____

____

____

____

____

____

____

____

____

Exercises:

Pain level
post exercise: _____

Date ________

Scale: _____ Sleep ______ Weight:______

Time/Temp: _______________

CC: ________________________

BM: _______________________

BP: _______________________

Rx: ______________________

Food/Drink:

Notes:

Exercises:

Pain level
post exercise: _____

"In three words I can sum up everything I've learned about life: it goes on."
—Robert Frost

Just for today I am thankful for

____

Date _________

Scale: _____ Sleep ______ Weight:______

Time/Temp: ________________

CC: ____________________________

BM: ____________________________

BP: ____________________________

Rx: ____________________________

Food/Drink:

Notes:

____

____

____

____

____

____

____

____

____

____

____

____

____

Exercises:

____

____

____

____

____

____

____

Pain level
post exercise: _____

____

Date _________

Scale: ______ Sleep _______ Weight:______

Time/Temp: ________________

CC: _____________________________

BM: _____________________________

BP: _____________________________

Rx: _____________________________

Notes:

____
____
____
____
____
____
____
____
____
____
____
____
____
____
____
____
____
____
____
____

Date _________

Scale: ______   Sleep _______   Weight:______

Time/Temp: _________________

CC: _______________________________

BM: ______________________________

BP: _________________________________

Rx: _________________________________

Food/Drink:

Notes:

____

____

____

____

____

____

____

____

____

____

____

____

____

____

____

____

____

____

____

Exercises:

**Pain level
post exercise:** ______

Date _________

Scale: ______ Sleep _______ Weight:_______

Time/Temp: __________________

CC: ___________________________

BM: _______________________________

BP: ____________________________

Rx: ____________________________

Notes:

____

____

____

____

____

____

____

____

____

____

____

____

____

____

____

____

____

____

____

____

____

Date _________

Scale: ______   Sleep _______   Weight:_______

Time/Temp: _________________

CC: _____________________________

BM: _____________________________

BP: _____________________________

Rx: _____________________________

Food/Drink:

Notes:

Exercises:

**Pain level
post exercise:** ______

Date _________

Scale: _____ Sleep ______ Weight:______

Time/Temp: _________________

CC: ___________________________

BM: ____________________________

BP: ____________________________

Rx: ____________________________

Food/Drink:

Notes:

____

____

____

____

____

____

____

____

____

____

____

____

____

____

____

Exercises:

____

____

____

____

____

____

Pain level
post exercise: _____

Date ________

Scale: _____ Sleep ______ Weight:______

Time/Temp: _______________

CC: _____________________________

BM: ____________________________

BP: ___________________________

Rx: ___________________________

Food/Drink:

Notes:

____

____

____

____

____

____

____

____

____

____

____

____

Exercises:

____

____

____

____

____

____

____

____

Pain level
post exercise: _____

____

Date _________

Scale: ______ Sleep _______ Weight:_______

Time/Temp: ________________

CC: _______________________

BM: _____________________________

BP: _______________________________

Rx: _______________________________

Food/Drink:

Notes:

____
____
____
____
____
____
____
____
____
____
____
____
____
____
____
____
____
____
____
____
____

Exercises:

Pain level
post exercise: ______

Date _________

Scale: ______ Sleep _______ Weight:_______

Time/Temp: _________________

CC: ___________________________

BM: _____________________________

BP: ______________________________

Rx: _______________________________

Food/Drink:

Notes:

Exercises:

Pain level
post exercise: ______

Who needs Jonathan!

Just for today I am thankful for

____

Date _________

Scale: ______   Sleep _______   Weight:_______

Time/Temp: _______________

CC: _______________________

BM: _____________________________

BP: ________________________________

Rx: ________________________________

Food/Drink:

Notes:

Exercises:

Pain level
post exercise: ______

Date ________

Scale: ______ Sleep ______ Weight:______

Time/Temp: ________________

CC: ____________________________

BM: ____________________________

BP: ______________________________

Rx: ____________________________

Food/Drink:

Notes:

____

____

____

____

____

____

____

____

____

____

____

Exercises:

____

____

____

____

____

____

____

____

____

Pain level
post exercise: ______

____

Date _________

Scale: ______ Sleep _______ Weight:_______

Time/Temp: _________________

CC: ________________________________

BM: _______________________________

BP: _______________________________

Rx: _______________________________

Food/Drink:

Notes:

____

____

____

____

____

____

____

____

____

____

____

____

____

____

____

____

____

____

____

Exercises:

Pain level
post exercise: ______

Date _________

Scale: ______ Sleep _______ Weight:_______

Time/Temp: ___________________

CC: _______________________________

BM: _______________________________

BP: _______________________________

Rx: _______________________________

Food/Drink:

Notes:

____

____

____

____

____

____

____

____

____

____

____

____

____

____

____

____

____

____

____

____

Exercises:

**Pain level
post exercise:** _____

Date ________

Scale: _____ Sleep _____ Weight:_____

Time/Temp: _______________

CC: _______________________

BM: _______________________

BP: _______________________

Rx: ____________________

Food/Drink:

Notes:

Exercises:

Pain level
post exercise: _____

Date _________

Scale: ______ Sleep ______ Weight:______

Time/Temp: _________________

CC: ___________________________

BM: _______________________________

BP: ___________________________

Rx: ___________________________

Food/Drink:

Notes:

____

____

____

____

____

____

____

____

____

____

____

____

Exercises:

____

____

____

____

____

____

____

____

Pain level
post exercise: ______

____

Date _________

Scale: ______   Sleep _______   Weight:______

Time/Temp: ________________

CC: ___________________________

BM: ______________________________

BP: _____________________________

Rx: _____________________________

Food/Drink:

Notes:

____
____
____
____
____
____
____
____
____
____
____
____
____
____
____
____
____
____
____
____

Exercises:

Pain level
post exercise: ______

Date _________

Scale: ______ Sleep ______ Weight:______

Time/Temp: __________________

CC: _______________________________

BM: ______________________________

BP: _______________________________

Rx: _______________________________

Food/Drink:

Notes:

____

____

____

____

____

____

____

____

____

____

____

____

____

____

____

____

____

____

____

____

Exercises:

Pain level
post exercise: ______

Date _________

Scale: ______   Sleep _______ Weight:______

Time/Temp: _________________

CC: _____________________________

BM: _______________________________

BP: _____________________________

Rx: _____________________________

Food/Drink:

Notes:

____

____

____

____

____

____

____

____

____

____

____

____

____

____

____

____

____

____

____

____

Exercises:

Pain level
post exercise: ______

"The simple act of paying attention can take you a long way."
—Keanu Reeves, Actor, 1964-present

Just for today I am thankful for

____

Date _________

Scale: _____ Sleep ______ Weight:______

Time/Temp: _______________

CC: _____________________

BM: _____________________

BP: _____________________

Rx: _____________________

Food/Drink:

Notes:

____
____
____
____
____
____
____
____
____
____
____
____
____
____
____
____
____
____
____
____
____

Exercises:

Pain level
post exercise: _____

Date _________

Scale: _____ Sleep ______ Weight:______

Time/Temp: _________________

CC: ______________________

BM: ____________________________

BP: ______________________________

Rx: ______________________________

Food/Drink:

Notes:

____

____

____

____

____

____

____

____

____

____

____

____

____

____

____

____

____

____

____

____

Exercises:

Pain level
post exercise: _____

Date _________

Scale: _____ Sleep ______ Weight:______

Time/Temp: ________________

CC: ____________________________

BM: ____________________________

BP: ____________________________

Rx: ____________________________

Food/Drink:

Notes:

____

____

____

____

____

____

____

____

____

____

____

____

____

____

____

____

____

____

____

Exercises:

Pain level
post exercise: _____

Date _________

Scale: _____ Sleep ______ Weight: ______

Time/Temp: _________________

CC: ____________________________

BM: _________________________

BP: ____________________________

Rx: ____________________________

Food/Drink:

Notes:

____

____

____

____

____

____

____

____

____

____

____

Exercises:

____

____

____

____

____

____

____

____

Pain level
post exercise: _____

____

Date ________ | Scale: _____ Sleep ______ Weight:______

Time/Temp: _______________ | CC: _______________________

BM: _______________________ | BP: _______________________

Rx: _______________________

Food/Drink:

Notes:

Exercises:

Pain level
post exercise: _____

Date _________

Scale: ______ Sleep _______ Weight: _______

Time/Temp: __________________

CC: ____________________________

BM: ______________________________

BP: ______________________________

Rx: ______________________________

Food/Drink:

Notes:

____

____

____

____

____

____

____

____

____

____

____

____

____

____

____

____

____

____

____

____

____

Exercises:

Pain level
post exercise: ______

Date ________

Scale: _____ Sleep ______ Weight:______

Time/Temp: _______________

CC: _________________________

BM: ________________________

BP: _________________________

Rx: ________________________

Food/Drink:

Notes:

Exercises:

Pain level
post exercise: _____

Date ________

Scale: _____ Sleep ______ Weight:______

Time/Temp: ________________

CC: ____________________________

BM: ____________________________

BP: ______________________________

Rx: ______________________________

Food/Drink:

Notes:

____

____

____

____

____

____

____

____

____

____

____

____

____

____

____

____

____

____

____

Exercises:

____

____

Pain level
post exercise: _____

Date _________

Scale: _____ Sleep ______ Weight:______

Time/Temp: ________________

CC: ___________________________

BM: ___________________________

BP: ___________________________

Rx: ___________________________

Food/Drink:

Notes:

____

____

____

____

____

____

____

____

____

____

____

____

____

Exercises:

____

____

____

____

____

____

____

Pain level
post exercise: _____

____

"I have not failed. I've just found 10,000 ways that won't work."
—Thomas A. Edison

Just for today I am thankful for

Date _________

Scale: ______ Sleep _______ Weight:______

Time/Temp: _________________

CC: ____________________________

BM: ____________________________

BP: ____________________________

Rx: ____________________________

Food/Drink:

Notes:

____

____

____

____

____

____

____

____

____

____

Exercises:

____

____

____

____

____

____

____

____

Pain level
post exercise: ______

____

Date _________

Scale: _____ Sleep _____ Weight:______

Time/Temp: ________________

CC: ___________________________

BM: ___________________________

BP: ___________________________

Rx: ___________________________

Food/Drink:

Notes:

____

____

____

____

____

____

____

____

____

____

____

____

____

____

____

____

____

____

____

____

____

Exercises:

Pain level
post exercise: _____

Date _________

Scale: _____ Sleep ______ Weight:______

Time/Temp: ________________

CC: ___________________________

BM: ______________________________

BP: ____________________________

Rx: ____________________________

Food/Drink:

Notes:

____

____

____

____

____

____

____

____

____

____

____

____

____

____

____

____

____

____

____

____

Exercises:

Pain level
post exercise: _____

Date _________

Scale: ______ Sleep _______ Weight:_______

Time/Temp: ________________

CC: ___________________________

BM: _______________________

BP: _____________________________

Rx: _____________________________

Food/Drink:

Notes:

____

____

____

____

____

____

____

____

____

____

____

____

____

____

____

____

____

____

____

____

Exercises:

Pain level
post exercise: ______

Date _________

Scale: ______   Sleep _______   Weight:______

Time/Temp: __________________

CC: ___________________________

BM: _______________________

BP: ____________________________

Rx: ___________________________

Food/Drink:

Notes:

____

____

____

____

____

____

____

____

____

____

____

____

____

____

____

____

____

____

____

____

Exercises:

Pain level
post exercise: ______

Date ________

Scale: ______ Sleep _______ Weight:______

Time/Temp: __________________

CC: ____________________________

BM: ______________________________

BP: ______________________________

Rx: ______________________________

Food/Drink:

Notes:

____
____
____
____
____
____
____
____
____
____
____
____
____
____
____
____
____
____
____

Exercises:

Pain level
post exercise: ______

Date _________

Scale: _____   Sleep ______   Weight:______

Time/Temp: ________________

CC: ___________________________

BM: _______________________

BP: ____________________________

Rx: ____________________________

Food/Drink:

Notes:

____

____

____

____

____

____

____

____

____

____

____

____

____

____

____

____

____

____

____

____

Exercises:

____

Pain level
post exercise: _____

Date _________

Scale: ______ Sleep _______ Weight:_______

Time/Temp: ________________

CC: _______________________________

BM: _______________________________

BP: _______________________________

Rx: _______________________________

Food/Drink:

Notes:

____

____

____

____

____

____

____

____

____

____

____

____

____

____

____

____

____

____

____

____

____

Exercises:

Pain level
post exercise: ______

Date ________

Scale: _____ Sleep ______ Weight:______

Time/Temp: ________________

CC: _________________________

BM: ___________________________

BP: _________________________

Rx: _________________________

Food/Drink:

Notes:

____

____

____

____

____

____

____

____

____

____

Exercises:

____

____

____

____

____

____

____

____

Pain level
post exercise: _____

Just for today I am thankful for

____

Date _________

Scale: _____ Sleep ______ Weight:______

Time/Temp: _______________

CC: ____________________

BM: _____________________

BP: _____________________

Rx: _____________________

Food/Drink:

Notes:

____

____

____

____

____

____

____

____

____

____

____

____

____

____

____

____

____

____

____

Exercises:

Pain level
post exercise: _____

Date _________

Scale: _____ Sleep ______ Weight:______

Time/Temp: _________________

CC: _____________________________

BM: _______________________________

BP: _______________________________

Rx: _______________________________

Food/Drink:

Notes:

____

____

____

____

____

____

____

____

____

____

____

____

____

____

____

____

____

____

____

____

Exercises:

Pain level
post exercise: _____

Date _________

Scale: ______ Sleep _______ Weight:_______

Time/Temp: __________________

CC: _____________________________

BM: _______________________

BP: ________________________________

Rx: ________________________________

Food/Drink:

Notes:

____

____

____

____

____

____

____

____

____

____

____

Exercises:

____

____

____

____

____

____

____

____

____

Pain level
post exercise: ______

____

Date _________

Scale: ______   Sleep _______   Weight:_______

Time/Temp: __________________

CC: _______________________

BM: ____________________________

BP: _______________________

Rx: _______________________

Notes:

____

____

____

____

____

____

____

____

____

____

____

____

____

____

____

____

____

____

____

____

Date ________

Scale: _____ Sleep ______ Weight:______

Time/Temp: ________________

CC: __________________________

BM: _________________________

BP: __________________________

Rx: __________________________

Food/Drink:

Notes:

Exercises:

Pain level
post exercise: _____

Date _________

Scale: ______ Sleep _______ Weight:_______

Time/Temp: _________________

CC: __________________________

BM: _____________________________

BP: _______________________________

Rx: _______________________________

Notes:

____

____

____

____

____

____

____

____

____

____

____

____

____

____

____

____

____

____

____

____

Exercises:

Pain level
post exercise: _____

Date _________

Scale: ______ Sleep _______ Weight:_______

Time/Temp: ________________

CC: _______________________________

BM: _______________________________

BP: _______________________________

Rx: _______________________________

Food/Drink:

Notes:

____

____

____

____

____

____

____

____

____

____

____

Exercises:

____

____

____

____

____

____

____

Pain level
post exercise: ______

____

Date _________

Scale: ______ Sleep _______ Weight:______

Time/Temp: ___________________

CC: ______________________________

BM: _______________________________

BP: ______________________________

Rx: ______________________________

Food/Drink:

Notes:

____

____

____

____

____

____

____

____

____

____

____

____

Exercises:

____

____

____

____

____

____

____

____

Pain level
post exercise: _____

____

Date _________

Scale: ______ Sleep _______ Weight:______

Time/Temp: ________________

CC: ____________________________

BM: _____________________________

BP: ______________________________

Rx: ______________________________

Food/Drink:

Notes:

____

____

____

____

____

____

____

____

____

____

____

____

____

____

____

____

____

____

____

Exercises:

Pain level
post exercise: ______

The glory to one is a glory to all

Just for today I am thankful for

____

Date _________

Scale: ______ Sleep _______ Weight:_______

Time/Temp: _________________

CC: ___________________________

BM: _______________________________

BP: _____________________________

Rx: _____________________________

Food/Drink:

Notes:

____

____

____

____

____

____

____

____

____

____

____

____

____

____

____

____

____

____

____

Exercises:

**Pain level
post exercise:** ______

Date _________

Scale: _____ Sleep ______ Weight:______

Time/Temp: ________________

CC: _____________________

BM: ______________________

BP: __________________

Rx: __________________

Food/Drink:

Notes:

____

____

____

____

____

____

____

____

____

____

____

____

____

____

Exercises:

____

____

____

____

____

____

____

Pain level
post exercise: _____

Date _________

Scale: _____ Sleep ______ Weight:______

Time/Temp: _______________

CC: ____________________________

BM: ____________________________

BP: ____________________________

Rx: ____________________________

Food/Drink:

Notes:

____

____

____

____

____

____

____

____

____

____

____

____

____

____

____

____

____

____

____

Exercises:

____

____

Pain level
post exercise: _____

Date ________

Scale: _____ Sleep ______ Weight:______

Time/Temp: ________________

CC: ____________________________

BM: _______________________

BP: ______________________________

Rx: ______________________________

Food/Drink:

Notes:

____

____

____

____

____

____

____

____

____

____

____

____

____

____

____

____

____

____

____

____

Exercises:

Pain level
post exercise: _____

Date _________

Scale: ______ Sleep _______ Weight:_______

Time/Temp: ________________

CC: _______________________________

BM: _______________________________

BP: _______________________________

Rx: _______________________________

Notes:

____

____

____

____

____

____

____

____

____

____

____

____

____

____

____

____

____

____

____

____

Date _________

Scale: ______ Sleep _______ Weight:______

Time/Temp: _________________

CC: _____________________________

BM: _______________________________

BP: _______________________________

Rx: _______________________________

Food/Drink:

Notes:

____

____

____

____

____

____

____

____

____

____

____

____

____

____

____

____

____

____

____

____

Exercises:

Pain level
post exercise: ______

Date _________

Scale: ______ Sleep ______ Weight:______

Time/Temp: ________________

CC: _____________________

BM: ____________________

BP: _____________________

Rx: _____________________

Food/Drink:

Notes:

Exercises:

Pain level
post exercise: ______

Date _________

Scale: ______   Sleep _______   Weight:_______

Time/Temp: ___________________

CC: _________________________________

BM: _______________________________

BP: _________________________________

Rx: ___________________________

Food/Drink:

Notes:

____

____

____

____

____

____

____

____

____

____

____

____

____

____

____

____

____

____

____

Exercises:

Pain level
post exercise: _____

Date _________

Scale: ______ Sleep _______ Weight:______

Time/Temp: _______________

CC: ____________________________

BM: ____________________________

BP: ____________________________

Rx: ____________________________

Food/Drink:

Notes:

____

____

____

____

____

____

____

____

____

____

____

____

____

____

____

____

____

____

____

____

____

Exercises:

Pain level
post exercise: ______

Just for today I am thankful for

____

Date _________

Scale: _____ Sleep ______ Weight:______

Time/Temp: _______________

CC: ____________________________

BM: ____________________________

BP: ____________________________

Rx: ____________________________

Food/Drink:

Notes:

____

____

____

____

____

____

____

____

____

____

____

Exercises:

____

____

____

____

____

____

____

Pain level
post exercise: _____

____

Date ________

Scale: _____ Sleep ______ Weight:______

Time/Temp: ________________

CC: ____________________________

BM: ____________________________

BP: ____________________________

Rx: ____________________________

Food/Drink:

Notes:

____

____

____

____

____

____

____

____

____

____

____

____

____

____

____

____

____

____

____

Exercises:

Pain level
post exercise: _____

Date _________

Scale: ______   Sleep _______   Weight:______

Time/Temp: ________________

CC: _________________________

BM: ___________________________

BP: ___________________________

Rx: ___________________________

Food/Drink:

Notes:

____

____

____

____

____

____

____

____

____

____

____

____

____

____

____

Exercises:

____

____

____

____

____

____

Pain level
post exercise: ______

Date __________

Scale: ______   Sleep _______   Weight:______

Time/Temp: _________________

CC: _______________________________

BM: _______________________________

BP: _______________________________

Rx: _______________________________

Food/Drink:

Notes:

____

____

____

____

____

____

____

____

____

____

____

____

____

____

____

____

____

____

____

____

Exercises:

Pain level
post exercise: ______

Date _________

Scale: _____ Sleep ______ Weight:______

Time/Temp: _______________

CC: ____________________________

BM: _____________________________

BP: _____________________________

Rx: _____________________________

Food/Drink:

Notes:

____

____

____

____

____

____

____

____

____

____

Exercises:

____

____

____

____

____

____

____

Pain level
post exercise: _____

____

Date _________

Scale: ______   Sleep _______   Weight:_______

Time/Temp: _________________

CC: __________________________

BM: ______________________________

BP: ___________________________

Rx: ____________________________

Food/Drink:

Notes:

Exercises:

Pain level
post exercise: ______

Date _________

Scale: ______ Sleep _______ Weight:______

Time/Temp: _________________

CC: _______________________________

BM: _______________________________

BP: _______________________________

Rx: _______________________________

Food/Drink:

Notes:

____

____

____

____

____

____

____

____

____

Exercises:

____

____

____

____

____

____

____

____

____

Pain level
post exercise: ______

____

Date _______

Scale: _____ Sleep ______ Weight:______

Time/Temp: ________________

CC: ____________________________

BM: ____________________________

BP: ____________________________

Rx: ____________________________

Food/Drink:

Notes:

____

____

____

____

____

____

____

____

____

____

____

____

____

____

____

____

____

____

____

____

Exercises:

**Pain level
post exercise:** _____

Date _________

Scale: _____   Sleep _____   Weight:______

Time/Temp: _______________

CC: ___________________________

BM: _____________________

BP: ____________________________

Rx: ___________________________

Food/Drink:

Notes:

____

____

____

____

____

____

____

____

____

____

____

Exercises:

____

____

____

____

____

____

____

____

____

Pain level
post exercise: _____

____

"Can I come in?"

Just for today I am thankful for

____

Date _________

Scale: _______ Sleep _______ Weight:_______

Time/Temp: _________________

CC: _________________________

BM: _____________________________

BP: _____________________________

Rx: _____________________________

Food/Drink:

Notes:

Exercises:

Pain level
post exercise: ______

Date ________   Scale: ____ Sleep _____ Weight:_____

Time/Temp: ______________   CC: ____________________

BM: ____________________   BP: ____________________

                     Rx: ____________________

Food/Drink: *Notes:*

Exercises:

Pain level post exercise: _____

Date _________

Scale: ______ Sleep _______ Weight:_______

Time/Temp: __________________

CC: _______________________________

BM: ________________________________

BP: ___________________________________

Rx: ___________________________________

Food/Drink:

Notes:

____

____

____

____

____

____

____

____

____

____

____

____

Exercises:

____

____

____

____

____

____

____

Pain level
post exercise: ______

____

Date _________

Scale: _____ Sleep ______ Weight:_______

Time/Temp: ________________

CC: _____________________________

BM: _____________________________

BP: _______________________________

Rx: ________________________________

Food/Drink:

Exercises:

**Pain level
post exercise:** _____

Notes:

____
____
____
____
____
____
____
____
____
____
____
____
____
____
____
____
____
____
____
____

Date _________

Scale: ______   Sleep _______ Weight:_______

Time/Temp: ________________

CC: _____________________________

BM: ____________________________

BP: ______________________________

Rx: ______________________________

Food/Drink:

Notes:

____

____

____

____

____

____

____

____

____

____

____

____

Exercises:

____

____

____

____

____

____

____

____

____

Pain level
post exercise: ______

____

Date _________

Scale: ______ Sleep _______ Weight:_______

Time/Temp: __________________

CC: ___________________________

BM: _______________________________

BP: ___________________________

Rx: ___________________________

Notes:

____

____

____

____

____

____

____

____

____

____

____

____

Exercises:

____

____

____

____

____

____

____

____

Pain level
post exercise: ______

____

Date _________

Scale: ______ Sleep _______ Weight:_______

Time/Temp: ___________________

CC: ______________________________

BM: _______________________________

BP: _________________________________

Rx: _________________________________

Food/Drink:

Notes:

____

____

____

____

____

____

____

____

____

____

____

Exercises:

____

____

____

____

____

____

____

Pain level
post exercise: ______

____

____

Date _________

Scale: _____ Sleep ______ Weight:______

Time/Temp: ________________

CC: ____________________________

BM: ______________________________

BP: ______________________________

Rx: ______________________________

Food/Drink:

Notes:

____

____

____

____

____

____

____

____

____

____

____

____

____

____

____

____

____

____

____

Exercises:

Pain level
post exercise: _____

Date _________

Scale: _____ Sleep ______ Weight:______

Time/Temp: ________________

CC: ___________________________

BM: _____________________________

BP: _____________________________

Rx: ___________________________

Food/Drink:

Notes:

____

____

____

____

____

____

____

____

____

____

____

____

____

____

____

____

____

____

Exercises:

Pain level
post exercise: _____

Keep on Smilin'

Just for today I am thankful for

____

Date ________

Scale: _____ Sleep ______ Weight:______

Time/Temp: _______________

CC: _______________________

BM: _________________________

BP: _______________________

Rx: _____________________

Food/Drink:

Notes:

Exercises:

**Pain level
post exercise:** _____

Date _________

Scale: ______   Sleep _______   Weight:_______

Time/Temp: _________________

CC: _______________________________

BM: _____________________________

BP: _______________________________

Rx: _______________________________

Food/Drink:

Notes:

____

____

____

____

____

____

____

____

____

____

____

____

____

____

____

____

____

____

____

____

Exercises:

Pain level
post exercise: _____

Date ________

Scale: _____ Sleep ______ Weight:______

Time/Temp: ________________

CC: _________________________

BM: ________________________

BP: _________________________

Rx: _________________________

Food/Drink:

Notes:

Exercises:

Pain level
post exercise: _____

Date _________

Scale: ______   Sleep _______   Weight:_______

Time/Temp: ________________

CC: ____________________________

BM: _______________________

BP: ______________________________

Rx: ______________________________

Food/Drink:

Notes:

Exercises:

Pain level
post exercise: ______

Date _________

Scale: ______ Sleep _______ Weight:_______

Time/Temp: _________________

CC: _____________________________

BM: ________________________________

BP: _________________________________

Rx: _________________________________

Food/Drink:

Notes:

____

____

____

____

____

____

____

____

____

____

____

____

Exercises:

____

____

____

____

____

____

____

Pain level
post exercise: ______

____

Date _________

Scale: ______ Sleep _______ Weight:_______

Time/Temp: ________________

CC: ____________________________

BM: ______________________________

BP: ______________________________

Rx: ______________________________

Food/Drink:

Notes:

Exercises:

Pain level
post exercise: ______

Date ________

Scale: _____ Sleep ______ Weight:______

Time/Temp: _______________

CC: _______________________

BM: _______________________

BP: _______________________

Rx: _______________________

Food/Drink:

Notes:

Exercises:

Pain level
post exercise: _____

Congratulations upon completing this
RecordKeeper.

Now it's time to order a new one.

One (or more) can be ordered by contacting me

at nedermarie@gmail.com, on amazon.com

or through my website, www.therecordkeeper.us

All images may be purchased through:

www.therecordkeeper.us – contact me via website

www.marie-neder.pixels.com – buy directly on the site

Please contact me for all inquiries at nedermarie@gmail.com

Thank you!

MEDICAL HISTORY

Current Physician Name/Number: _____________________ (___) ___-____
Current Pharmacy Name/Number: _____________________ (___) ___-____

CURRENT/PAST MEDICATIONS

name	dose	frequency	starting	ending	physician	purpose

SURGICAL PROCEDURES

date	procedure	physician	hospital	notes

MAJOR ILLNESSES

illness	start	end	physician	treatment notes

VACCINATIONS

name	date	name	date
tetanus		meningitis	
influenza vaccine		yellow fever	
Zostavax		polio	
other vaccine		other vaccine	

<table><tr><td colspan="2">Emergency Contact Form</td></tr></table>

Ensure that the information on this form is validated and updated periodically.

Personal Information	Date when this form was filled or updated:

Name: ____

Work Address: ____

____

____
   City   State   Zip code

Home Address: ________________________________ ____________________

____
   City   State   Zip code

Home Phone: _______________ Work Phone: ________________ Cell Phone: _______________

E-mail (Home): ___________________________ E-mail (Work): ___________________________

Primary person to be notified in case of an emergency:

Name: ____

Relationship: Relative ______________ Friend ______________ Other ______________

Home Address: ____
    Street Address   City   State   Zip code

Home Phone: _______________ Work Phone: ________________ Cell Phone: _______________

E-mail Address: ____

Secondary person to be notified in case of an emergency:

Name: ____

Relationship: Relative ______________ Friend ______________ Other ______________

Home Address: ____
    Street Address   City   State   Zip code

Home Phone: _______________ Work Phone: ________________ Cell Phone: _______________

E-mail Address: ____

You can download these forms on freeprintablemedicalforms.com

Image Titles

These images may be purchased through:
www.therecordkeeper.us
www.marie-neder.pixels.com

Please contact me for all inquiries at nedermarie@gmail.com

Acknowledgments

First and foremost I want to thank and acknowledge those who
supported me with the first "The RecordKeeper" that was published in
April of 2017. They are:

E Bender-Webb for his friendship, creative spirit and emotional support
during this wonderful adventure; Doranne Long for her support,
friendship and book creation suggestions; Sue Jordan, my friend,
fellow photographer and my weekly walking partner.

Others whose privacy I want to protect: Kathy, Lanette, Kelly, Julie,
Michael, and Ashley – to name just a few.

Last, but certainly not least: Deborah Perdue with
illuminationgraphics.com who has guided me through this awesome
process of bringing to fruition *The RecordKeeper*. Her skills were
once again utilized for this second book titled
The RecordKeeper – Another pathway to greater well-being.

.

Did I mention a higher power? Can't forget that for this second book
as well. This spark, mojo, energy, creativity, humor,
and humility has enabled me to bring
The RecordKeeper – Another pathway to greater well-being to life.

Thank you one and all.

Marie

Made in the USA
Monee, IL
07 July 2026

56551679R00125